From the Desk of Tucson Poetry Society

2020 Visions

Published on behalf of Tucson Poetry Society. Copyrights retained by individual poets.

Alan Perry's poem "COVID Wing—Day 97" first appeared in *Global Poemic*, Sep. 2020.
Gene Twaronite's poem "Social Distance" first appeared in *Evening Street Review*.
Gene Twaronite's poem "Journey by Layers" first appeared in *Fourteen Hills*.

Interior design by Wynne Brown LLC.
Cover design by Brad Peterson.

Lyric Power
Tucson, Arizona

With Gratitude

To all who participated in this project reflecting on the year 2020

To the poets who shared their works

To the illustrator and editor, Bradley N. Peterson, aka Anderson Atlas

To the editor, Wynne Brown

To the committee: Hank Dallago, Sandra Luber, Alan Perry, Elaine A. Powers, and Nan Rubin

And to all whose lives are touched by poetry

Contents

Lori Bonati	8
Dianne Brown	10
Hank Dallago	12
Colleen Eichenberger	14
Anita Fonte	16
Janice Fuller	18
Mark Hudson	20
Frank Iosue	22
Linda LaVere	24
Sandra Luber	26
Constance Marconi	28
Alan Perry	30
Elaine A. Powers	32
Janet McMillan Rives	34
Patty Robertson	36
Nan Rubin	38
Jon Sebba	40
Gene Twaronite	42
Joy Valerius	44
David Van Houten	46
Stuart Watkins	48
Sarah Zale	50

Lori Bonati

Lori Bonati is a retired school psychologist who finds joy in writing, photography, music, and the great outdoors. Currently, she is working on a middle-grade novel, a book of poems paired with photographs, a children's picture book, and a cookbook. loristory.wordpress.com

National Debt

Snowflakes drop like loose change
through holes in tattered clouds
and are deposited on the unemployed
who wait in line at the food bank
spangling heads with silver
dotting hoodies with stars
slipping into empty pockets
melting

Across the street, a grey sedan
glides into the teller lane
lowers a tinted window
extends a cashmere sleeve and leather glove
a stack of bills appears in a gleaming tray
cash is quietly counted
as the car idles like a well-fed cat
purring

Satisfied, the driver heads for home
past the row of those who've slept in cars
or risen from perilous sidewalks
they are draped in banners of bright stars
broad stripes furrow their brows
they'll return by the dawn's early light
owing much in this land of the free
drowning

Dianne Brown

Dianne Brown resides in Wellton, Arizona, with her husband Rich. Poetry has been a part of her life since her adolescent years. She has published, through a grant, a chapbook of poetry entitled "Catching Colors." A twenty-year-after sequel is in the making to be titled "Colors Caught." At present, Dianne is the ASPS Member-Contest Coordinator and looks forward to the adventure.

Winter, Spring, Summer

The sky is gray
The air is cold
The wet will
Never dry
Until my colors
Rise and touch
The soggy
Winter sky.

Spring is in bloom
Nests in construction
Inhale the day
Deeply smell May
Blue brain-freeze skies
Arms open wide
Hum a red-robin tune
Sing amore to June

The sun turns
Hay rolls into
Golden spun buns
Lolling about
Meadow grasses
Van Gogh-ing
My eyes with
Summer's bright strokes

Hank Dallago

Poet and children's picture book writer, Hank worked in the financial services field by day and was an accomplished percussionist by night. He uses grammar artistically to frame a rhythmic and lyrical experience, using language and form in creative ways, touching the readers' emotions and exciting imaginations.

Ghost Light

Dedicated to all theatre productions that will triumphantly return to sold out shows after the pandemic.

Bright as a klieg light:
searching a barren stage
exposing abandoned house
averting tragic accidents
exposing unruly spirits
sanctuary to exited
characters'
lone
act.

Light bulb
flashes to recall
performers' voices
animated expressions
emotions mirrored
in the audience
set in the
dark so
act
can
go
on!

Colleen Eichenberger

Colleen is a "snowbird" and lifelong arts enthusiast/advocate who enjoys Arizona winters and Minnesota summers especially when working on a poem or fine-tuning an abstract painting. Mostly, she goes for the moment of inspiration that can hit when steeped in any creative endeavor.

Poet

It's a simple faith, really
no waving of palms
few, if any Hosannas
hardly ever coming undone

I admit the walk ordinary
through valleys and shadows
seldom fearing evil alone
as you know, I travel light

Mostly like you
sitting there on task
working late as usual
going with the flow.

Sheila

You lovely
Jamaican pearl
woman of elegance
proper mind of God's calm.

Thank You, Smooth Mother
so cool like balm
you soothe
Divine.

Anita Fonte

Anita has been writing poems since elementary school and published a few in college. In between four decades of education and community development work, she published a dissertation from University of Arizona, two self-published books (nonfiction and a collection of flash fiction), newspaper and national journal articles and always penned poems via social media. Lately, children's literature is her new creative adventure.

Two in Partial Isolation

My home is my snuggery.
Sunshine peeks through the curtains.
Birdsongs prod me to shuffle outside,
Pour the seeds and water sturdy flowers.
If I tend to both, they return the comfort tenfold.

After a rainy day
The desert air blooms with lightness,
Purple flowers cover stubby bushes
Like a lavender blanket,
Finches reappear for sunflower seeds
Scattered outside the window.

Janice Fuller

Janice S Fuller is a poet who lives and writes in the desert of Tucson, Arizona, and on a lake in Wisconsin. Her poems have been published in *Caesura*, *Amsterdam Quarterly*, and *Gyroscope Review* among others. She's lucky enough to have both loons and saguaros to inspire her.

One More Thing

It's been one thing after another.
First the virus, then the
tumors, the death and
protests. Now the fire on
the mountain.

What next?
Vampires run
through the
Sonoran Desert?
Floods rush down the
mountain? Trees all fall
down gagging on the
noxious air? The sun gives
up shining? Or the Apple
Store closes just when your
iPhone quits. Maybe the
Russians finally hack the
internet, turn it off.

But did I tell you all
the hopeful things
that elbowed their
way into the chaos?
Like Baby Harry's
arrival. Or none of our
kids losing their jobs.
The promise to fix this
country's failures, make
equality a *real* thing.
Young people, all colors,
marching, fed up with
lives that haven't
mattered.
And then there's the flowering
Red Bird of Paradise framing every roadside.

Mark Hudson

Mark is a frequently published poet and writer. His poetry can be found at illinoispoets.org

My Muse Did Not Die

Corona virus was in the news; but
one thing that didn't die was my
muse.
By nature, everything is an inspiration,
I remained calm during the devastation.
I was inspired by children and birds,
birds singing songs inspired my words.
Children's upbeat attitude brought
cheer, even though secretly I felt some
fear. My God didn't want me to be
alarmed, even though many people had
been harmed. I became used to my mask
adorning my face, as my glasses
steamed up, I slowed my pace. I tried to
go for walks, thinking of verses, but
everything around me brought
out curses. People everywhere, six feet
apart, oh death! Don't you have a heart?
I learned how to connect to people
with Zoom, seeing all the people I love in my
room. It was like watching TV, but my friends
the hosts, and in my town, the
world was full of ghosts. Businesses
shut down, windows boarded,
selfishness, many groceries hoarded.
Still, the sun still was able to shine often,
unseen by those who went to their
coffin. But I believe in eternity, in a holy
creator, we will hopefully meet him
sooner or later.
And if we transcend to paradise, we will be glad,
that is why nothing can make me too sad.

Frank Iosue

Frank Iosue holds a B. A. in English from Cal State L.A., and an M. F. A. in Creative Writing / Poetry from the University of Iowa / Writer's Workshop. His volume of collected poems, *The Au Revoir Of An Enormous Us*, was published in 2017 and is available at Amazon.com.

Freudian Episode

She shuts the drapes and turns to her lover
standing naked at the other end of the room.
This is the jungle of the mirror, and the air
is a deep ether of powders and perfumes.

Her body is arboreal and damp, and, at his touch,
quivers like a frond of fern. The scent of her pumps
in and out of his lungs. It's terrible to be beasts
like this. Passion grows hideous and elephantine.

They slide up against each other like osmotic slugs,
and feed until they are each other and out of reach.
In bed, they are obese. When they are done, they sleep
uneasily through the afternoon and dream; dream

of a place where animals are happy, and friends
with what they eat. But, outside, birds peck and twitter
erratically in the trees, and squirrels claw and kick
their way across the lawn like insatiable, agitated toys.

An Enlightenment

Seek greater knowledge.
Live more intelligently.
Die better informed.

To Be Always A God

The stars are my eyes.
The planets, all darknesses,
my periphery.

Linda LaVere

Linda LaVere is the daughter of World War II veterans, trained and educated by mentors Glover Davis and Denise Levertov and an editor for *Eye Prayers*, a national poetry magazine. She was also a musician who sang show tunes and Irish folksongs in full costume at Renaissance fairs, in restaurants, for mayors and the submarine fleet in San Diego. Her two books: *Bridge of Bones*, and *Shadowlands* can be found on Amazon.

A Buddhist at the Watering Can

A flying insect has drowned
itself in the watering can.
The wings float, laid out on the
surface like the arranged hair on the
pillow of a planned suicide. She is in
full make-up with fake eyelashes and
her loveliest dress, more like a dead
fairy than a delicate bug.

I think about removing the one I name
Scarlet from the water, but can't think
where I would put the body.
No one will come to claim the
remains or plant a cross over the
mound of earth, or wail at my
door.
Whistling a little dirge in her honor,
I leave her to it, pour a
little death onto the
flowers with their
morning drink.

There are no real solutions.

Sandra Luber

A retired Hollywood film editor, Sandra Luber is the writer of *Divine Intercourse*, and three creative nonfiction works. Her published poems appear in the *Tucson Poetry Society Anthology 2019*, *Betterthanstarbucks*, and *Metaforologia*. Her poetry fuses philosophy with a message of unity, inspired by her Buddhist practice. She resides happily in Tucson, Arizona.

One-Part Harmony

I hear your wild whispers rush
to embrace rock after rock
smoothing the roughest with love
I hear you touching echo dreams
playing loops of laughter
childhood innocence
born of the universe
singing our song

In you, dear earth
I see the cosmos
lakes and rivers nourishing
    the tiniest daisy,
lusty sunsets, lingering moonsets
leave me aching
if you survive
    we survive
how beautiful together
    we are

I bow grateful to
sun, soil, rain, wind
    making you visible
        and
praise the petals
    of your heart

Constance Marconi

Constance Marconi has self-published a book about the summer desert, "Was That A Breeze?" After her first grandchild was born 18 years ago, she became one of the first early grandparent bloggers creating 'Play Wit Me Nana.' Constance (also known as Connie) loves to write poems and has recently picked up the guitar with plans to do some songwriting. She is an RN and has a career in the Acute Inpatient Rehabilitation Hospital setting, which has also been inspiration for her writing.

Selfie with my Granddaughter

At the farmers market
across from the dusty horse track
beside the dry river bed
on a concrete bench

you tilt
your iPhone camera
pursue the perfect angle
on your ten dollar Acai bowl
and us

the cold purple foreign fruit
pulped high
sprinkled up to the minute
in organic coconut
glory be to this moment
frozen in scene

you ripening to a teenager
and me
blossoming
to a prune.

Alan Perry

Alan Perry's debut poetry chapbook, *Clerk of the Dead*, was published by Main Street Rag Publishing in 2020. His poems have appeared or are forthcoming in *Tahoma Literary Review, Heron Tree, Open: Journal of Arts & Letters, Broadkill Review* and elsewhere, and in several anthologies. He is a Senior Poetry Editor for *Typehouse Literary Magazine*, a Best of the Net nominee, and holds a BA in English from the University of Minnesota. More at: https://AlanPerryPoetry.com

COVID Wing—Day 97

Lines on her face
trace the straps she curls
over her ears, tightening
the medicinal-smelling mask
around her nose, across her cheeks
under her chin. A face shield
tightly banded on her forehead
reflects what lies in front of her.
Hard to breathe, harder still
for her patients, their lines
in the hall grow longer each day.
More tubing to connect, intubations
to perform, rotation of the dead
with the near-dying--hallway
to room to hallway, and again.
Her voice is muffled as she holds
an iPad in front of the patient
encouraging his relatives to say
words she's heard before.
No one can read her face
under the mask, the turning corners
of her mouth as breath fades
biting her lip when the patient
no longer inhales.
Droplets run past her nose
into the absorbent mask.
Her goggles fog up
from the heat, the heaviness
of what she must wear.

Elaine A. Powers

Elaine A. Powers is a retired biologist, who now writes rhyming science-based children's picture books. Originally from Peoria, IL, Elaine lives in Oro Valley, AZ, with her muses: iguanas, tortoises and turtles. Elaine is the President of the Tucson Poetry Society and Vice President of the Arizona State Poetry Society.
www.elaineapowers.com
www.lyricpower.net
https://www.facebook.com/elaine.powers.50

Welcome to my Corona World
(Corona Virus Disease - 19)

Although my name is like a beer,
No social drink has brought me here.
The environment was stressed by man
And that's how my release began.
In bats' immune systems, I was supercharged,
And thus my world became enlarged.
How do I move from place to place?
As an aerosol, I land on your face.
Just breathe me in or touch your eyes,
Then you're infected, you'll realize.
I bind to cells with ACE-2,
Does that mean anything to you?
I get inside and settle in,
Then start making bradykinin.
I cause your blood vessels to leak,
Then into your tissues I can sneak.
I induce hyaluronic acid as well,
Turning fluid in lungs into hydrogel.
Some scientists say I'm not alive,
Because I require other cells to survive.
But with my replication method,
No need for genetic mating is accepted.
You may think vaccines will seal my fate,
But as a virus, I can often mutate.
So new variants I will produce
As I replicate and reproduce.
I've changed the body's world from within,
Now changing the world without can begin.
My abilities are now unfurled
And I am able to conquer the world.

Janet McMillan Rives

Janet McMillan Rives resides in Tucson, Arizona. Her poetry has appeared in such journals as *Lyrical Iowa, Raw Art Review, Ekphrastic Review, Heirlock, Sandcutters, The Blue Guitar,* and *Fine Lines*. Her chapbook, *Into This Sea of Green: Poems from the Prairie*, was published in 2020. http://www.janetmrives.com

On Horsebarn Hill

At nine I knew what happy meant—
the opposite of bustling, the slow pace
of a one-stop-light town, even slower
on the edge, no neighbors, just four of us
each finding our way in a rented farm house

horses nickering their joy
in the riding ring next door, cows
mooing, chewing in the pasture,
pigs, an oink, a squeal, a grunt

the red barn up the hill, the bluest
summer sky, a blinding yellow sun,
then blue mixed with yellow making
green everywhere—maples, pines,
hills, ivy trellised wall paper,
two-toned Ford, mint and evergreen,
out back Mother's glads bursting
into every vibrant shade of gold,
orange, purple, burgundy

pot roast in the oven, angel food cake
cooling on the kitchen table, carrots
straight from the garden, ice cream
for ten cents fresh from the college dairy.

At nine I knew what happy meant
yet how strange to find it today—quiet
moments in self quarantine, sounds of birds,
wind, the scent of rain, a world alive—
unexpected gifts of human isolation.

Patty Robertson

Patty Robertson is the author of *Jane Austen's Imagination: lyrical expressions*, a collection of original poetry on the life and works of Jane Austen, her second Austen-related book. *With Bronte Intensity: expressive contemplations*, her second collection of poetry based on the life and works of the Bronte family is forthcoming. Patty enjoys time with family, reading, and music, and lives in Vail, Arizona.

Curiously
Ominous
Metaphysical
Assessment

global trauma strikes, paralyzing shock
hypoxia threatens human life with
prolonged mist of unconsciousness

primal reflexes amid pandemic restrictions
fear of disease, irregular panting behind
masks yawn of listless disconnection, inert
exhaustion

approaching institutional footsteps trigger
involuntary mumbling of masses impaired
memories of former freedoms falter
confusion pervades where truth is
suppressed distorted, twisted anarchical
powers push prone impassive bodies
whose eyes fail to open

stupors continue until the silent surface ripples
emerging from enforced stillness latent struggles
rise to exhale autonomous fiery breath

Nan Rubin

Nan Rubin is a retired psychotherapist and artist. Her debut poetry book, *Encounters, Inspiration from the Natural World*, published in 2016 by Wheatmark Press, can be found on Amazon. Her poetry is also included in *KYSO Flash Anthology, Volume I, Knock-Your Socks-Off Art and Literature*.

Thawed By Love

In the swirling vapor of my freezer, I glimpse Grandma a few inches tall covered in freezer burn.
Pointing her finger, she laments: *All anyone will talk about at my funeral are these meals I cooked and froze for all of you as my "thanks" for those quick family visits.*

We all traveled home with her plastic containers of culinary gold: rugelach raisin nut pastries size of a man's thumb, savory sweet and sour meatballs, rolled cabbage spiked with ginger, and chicken soup laced with parsnip, carrots, and dill – roto-rooter for congestion, her loneliness and longing released in its steamy vapors.

I can see her rolling out noodle dough, chopping onions, eyes tearing, sweeping and scrubbing floors, meals cooked, endlessly served to her husband, the plumber of stocky build and few words who failed to hug her unless told to.

Always, I traveled home with my own cache of gold, but not before anointing her with love:

I'd lift those empty arms to encircle me, enfold her in mine, then a nuzzle and deposit of kisses into that wrinkled neck, dusty from face powder. We'd stand bosom to bosom until she finally giggled and softened like a cooked noodle.

Jon Sebba

Jon Sebba, a left-brained engineer for forty years, is a combat veteran with mild PTSD. He tries to show veterans and other sufferers how poetry helped him address his stress demons. He and his wife live between two poetry Meccas: Salt Lake City, Utah, and Tucson, Arizona, and shuttle back and forth in harmony with the seasons.
http://yossiyassersoldiers.wix.com/yossi-yasser

Low-level Poet

Everything's nearer, nine inches off the sidewalk.
Her senses focus on details—eyes, ears, nose
all her faculties in play. She notices.

A blemish in the concrete, shoeprints
on a moist lawn, wet paw prints in gutter,
gum wrapper, bird splat noted and assessed.

She catalogues the scent of one cat and a million
fresh-mown blades of grass, with a tinge of engine oil,
in sharp contrast to the cut of a spark-spitting edger.

A night-crawler desperately struggles to return
to its damp dark sanctuary, from which it fled
during the quarter-inch flood that lasted a worm-
month.

In the dawn, my terrier freezes, her tail
as straight as she can manage, her nose
and ears point toward a potential threat—

a red fire-hydrant. Driven by a malamute-scent,
she trots past the two-armed menace in search
of another pair of early-bird walkers.

She practices the rules of good writers:
listen, be aware and surprised,
touch, smell, savor and witness,
be in awe, entranced and inspired,
by everything.

Gene Twaronite

Gene Twaronite's first poetry book *Trash Picker on Mars* (Kelsay Books) was the winner of the 2017 New Mexico-Arizona Book Award for Arizona poetry. His latest collections are *The Museum of Unwearable Shoes* and *What the Gargoyle Sees*. Follow him at: www.thetwaronitezone.com

Social Distance

The distance from grip to the stinging tip of a bullwhip
The distance between two arms spread wide
The distance in which two breaths mingle
The distance to the end of a leash
The distance across that door at the end of Titanic
The distance growing like continental drift
The distance to the next island country of one

Journey by Layers

We journey by layers, first the
outer skin is shed, serpent-wise,
leaving behind all schedules,
rituals and detritus of daily life to
scatter in the wake of our
departure.

At each destination, we
peel away another
layer, losing ourselves
by degree in going
from here to there,
leaving a trail of things
we thought essential
until at last we arrive,
our suitcase in tatters.

Better not to open it.

Joy Valerius

Joy Valerius graduated from the University of Arizona and has been writing poetry for over 30 years. She published a collection of dog poems titled "Dogs on the Verge of Poetry" which is available at Amazon.com. She is often inspired by her Poetry Pups who eat up her poems as if they were tasty bones. www.JoyValerius.com

Sheltering at Home

Shelter at home?
Why that's as good

as a bone
my dog says to me.

It won't be hard
to comply,

I'll happily keep my eye
on you,

chase the virus
away if it comes for you.

Home is heaven
as our time together

explodes. Working
from home

neither of us
will be alone.

David Van Houten

A retired educator of young children, David moved from Michigan to Tucson with his husband Steve in 2010. He began writing poetry in earnest with instructor Dan Gilmore at the Osher Lifelong Learning Institute at the University of Arizona in 2015. Gilmore's passion for poetry convinced him that the challenges of composing poems are well worth the rewards. David's work has been published in the *Oasis Journal 2017*.

breathe

beside a dry river wash
stands a grove of desert pines

steadfast trunks rise from roots
braided deep within the earth

branches stretch overhead
arc in full canopy

offer shelter from relentless heat
amid streams of filtered sunlight

ground dense with needlework
no footstep is heard

boughs beckon in the breeze
move me to pause

ease into their embrace
accept their generosity

surrender
to shaded sanctuary

Stuart Watkins

Stuart Watkins: retired teacher, active poet, writer, publisher, plays POP tennis, hikes, and loves the outdoors. Married with three adult children, two grandchildren, and enjoying life.

You Know of Whom I Speak.

When I was walking in the desert and a thorn
from a mesquite tree scratched my arm,
I thought of the one who had a crown of thorns set
upon His head.
You know of whom I speak.
When I climbed the Catalina Mountains
for six and a half
long hours up and down running out of water and
praying to make it home,
I thought of the one who spent forty days
in the wilderness.
You know of whom I speak.
A thorn pierced my tennis shoe, not wise to have
worn, and lodged in my big toe and pulling it out
was a hurtful act.
I thought of the one who had spikes hammered
into His hands and feet.
You know of whom I speak.
My desert hike ended in making it home
exhausted, thirsty, tired and weak, but
somehow stronger in faith remembering
Him
Who endured it all for me.

You know of whom I speak.

Sarah Zale

Sarah Zale teaches writing and works on Art for Justice projects. Her first book, *The Art of Folding: Poems* (2010) was inspired by travels to Israel and Palestine. *Sometimes You Do Things* highlights the history of Detroit and celebrates its rebuilding. Her publishing company, Wildflower Press, has released the anthology *Strange Fruit: Poems on the Death Penalty* (2019).

Wonder in the Time of Virus

disconnected from everything, she dares not
touch the beetle (on its back, its legs spinning)

she has forgotten what she planned to do today
that one just one thing only it is hard to recall
why it matters

she stands, steps, stops
unsteady without a reason she can name
as a spider crosses her path

the spider's legs: angular lines, waves
of a heartbeat, quicken with a fear
of her vagary to rid it from this world

she loses herself in a digital clock,
waiting for a minute to pass, trying
to remember before, trying to imagine after

her gaze drifts toward something wild, rosy faced—
a lovebird in flight from a foxtail palm
to the torches in bloom on an ocotillo

it is a wonder—
a trill of notes, uncaged,
that punctures the air and escapes on a breeze

she catches the song on her lips
and sends it out again.

Made in the USA
Middletown, DE
08 July 2021